The ESS  of

THERMODYNAMICS I

Staff of Research and Education Association,
Dr. M. Fogiel, Director

This book covers the usual course outline of Thermodynamics I. For more advanced topics, see *"THE ESSENTIALS OF THERMODYNAMICS II"*.

 Research and Education Association
61 Ethel Road West
Piscataway, New Jersey 08854

THE ESSENTIALS OF THERMODYNAMICS I

Printed in the United States of America

Library of Congress Catalog Card Number 87-61802

International Standard Book Number 0-87891-626-1

WHAT "THE ESSENTIALS" WILL DO FOR YOU

This book is a review and study guide. It is comprehensive and it is concise.

It helps in preparing for exams, in doing homework, and remains a handy reference source at all times.

It condenses the vast amount of detail characteristic of the subject matter and summarizes the **essentials** of the field.

It will thus save hours of study and preparation time.

The book provides quick access to the important facts, principles, theorems, concepts, and equations of the field.

Materials needed for exams, can be reviewed in summary form — eliminating the need to read and re-read many pages of textbook and class notes. The summaries will even tend to bring detail to mind that had been previously read or noted.

This "ESSENTIALS" book has been carefully prepared by educators and professionals and was subsequently reviewed by another group of editors to assure accuracy and maximum usefulness.

Dr. Max Fogiel
Program Director

CONTENTS

CHAPTER 1

BASIC CONCEPTS

1.1 THERMODYNAMIC SYSTEMS

The term system as used in thermodynamics refers to a definite quantity of matter bounded by some closed surface which is impervious to the flow of matter. This surface is called the boundary of the system. Everything outside the boundary of a system constitutes it surroundings.

Depending on the nature of the boundary involved, we can classify a thermodynamic system in one of the following three categories:

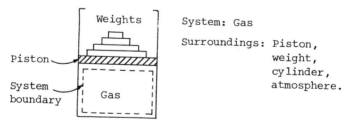

System: Gas

Surroundings: Piston,
weight,
cylinder,
atmosphere.

Fig. 1.1 Example of a system

a) An Isolated System allows neither heat nor work transfer across the boundary.

b) An Open System allows exchange of both matter and energy.

c) A Closed System allows only exchange of energy.

1.2 PROPERTIES OF SYSTEMS

The state of a system is its condition as identified by coordinates which can usually be observed quantitatively, such as volume, density, temperature, etc. These coordinates are called properties.

All properties of a system can be divided into two types:

a) An Intensive Property is independent of the mass. (Pressure, density, temperature)

b) An extensive property has a value which varies directly with the mass. (Volume, energy, entropy)

1.3 PROCESSES

When a thermodynamic system changes from one state to another, it is said to execute a process, which is described in terms of the end states. A cycle is a process in which the end states are identical.

Processes are classified according to the following categories:

a) An Isothermal Process is a constant-temperature process.

b) An Isobaric Process is a constant-pressure process.

c) An Isometric Process is a constant-volume process.

d) An Adiabatic Process is a process in which heat does not cross the system boundary.

e) A Quasistatic Process consists of a succession of equilibrium states, such that at every instant the system involved departs only from the equilibrium state.

f) In a Reversible Process, the initial state of the system involved can be restored with no observable effects in the system and its surroundings. This is called an Ideal Process.

g) In an Irreversible Process, the initial state of the system involved cannot be restored without observable effects in the system and its surroundings.

1.4 THERMODYNAMIC EQUILIBRIUM

When a system is not subject to interactions and a change of state cannot occur, then the system is in a state of equilibrium. There are four kinds of equilibrium: stable, neutral, unstable and metastable. Of these, a stable equilibrium is the one most encountered in thermodynamics. A system is in a state of stable equilibrium if a finite change of state of the system cannot occur without leaving a corresponding, finite alteration in the state of the environment. Figure 1.2, of a marble at rest in a covered bowl is an example of such a state. To have thermodynamic equilibrium, the conditions of mechanical, chemical and thermal equilibrium must be satisfied.

Fig. 1.2

A system is in mechanical equilibrium when it has no unbalanced force within it and when the force it exerts on its boundary is balanced by external forces.

A system is in thermal equilibrium when its temperature is uniform throughout, and equal to the temperature of the surroundings.

A system is in chemical equilibrium when the chemical composition of the system remains unchanged.

1.5 MUTUAL EQUILIBRIUM

Two systems are in mutual equilibrium if they are brought into communication and there is no change in either system.

1.6 ZEROTH LAW OF THERMODYNAMICS

When two systems are each in thermal equilibrium with a third system, they are also in thermal equilibrium with each other.

1.7 PRESSURE

Pressure is defined as the force per unit area on a surface whose dimensions are large, or

$$P = \frac{F}{A}$$

where

P = Pressure,   F = Normal force on the area element A.

Pressure as defined above is called the absolute pressure. Most pressure gauges read the difference between the absolute pressure in a system and the absolute pressure of the atmosphere. This difference is called the gauge pressure. Relations between these pressures are shown in Fig. 1.3.

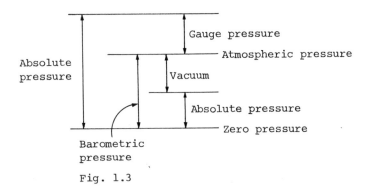

Fig. 1.3

4

1.7.1 UNITS OF PRESSURE

(I) Engineering system: One pound force per square foot (lbf/ft^2)

(II) International system: (a) Pascal (Pa) = 1 N/M^2 (1.1)
                                    (b) 1 bar = 10^{5}Pa = 0.1 MPa   (1.2)

A pressure of one standard atmosphere is defined as the pressure produced by a column of mercury exactly 76 cm in length, of density 13.5951 gm/cm^3 at a point where g is 980.665 cm/sec^2.

$$1 \text{ standard atmosphere} = 1.01324 \times 10^6 \ \frac{\text{dynes}}{\text{cm}^2} = 14.6959 \text{ lb/in}^2$$

1.8 OTHER PROPERTIES

a) Average specific volume: $\bar{v} = \dfrac{V}{m}$ (1.3)
where

       V = Total volume of the system
       m = Total mass of the system

b) The average density ρ of a system is the reciprocal of of the average specific volume, or

$$\boxed{\bar{\rho} = \frac{1}{\bar{v}} = \frac{m}{V}}$$

                                                       (1.4)

c) A specific value of a property can be defined at each point of a system as the average specific value of the property in a physically infinitesimal volume element that includes the point.

(I) Specific volume = $\dfrac{dV}{dm}$ (1.5)

(II) Density = $\dfrac{1}{v} = \dfrac{dm}{dV}$ (1.6)

5

1.9 DIMENSIONS AND UNITS

Dimensions are names given to physical quantities. Some examples of dimensions are length, time, mass, force, volume and velocity.

A unit is a definite standard or measure of a dimension. For example, foot, meters and angstroms are all different units of the common dimension of length.

There are four systems of international units:

a) International system

b) English Engineering System

c) Absolute engineering system

d) Absolute metric system

The dimensions and units of the four basic systems are summarized in table 1.

Dimensions and Units of Different Dimensional Systems

Name of System	Primary Quantities			Derived Quantities			g_c in $F = \frac{1}{g_c} ma$
	Mass	Length	Time	Force	Mass	Force	
SI	kg	m	s	—	—	N	$g_c = 1$
English engineering	lbm	ft	s	lbf	—	—	$g_c = 32.174 \frac{\text{ft-lbm}}{\text{lbf-s}^2}$
Absolute engineering	—	ft	s	lbf	slug	—	$g_c = 1$
Absolute metric (cgs)	gm	cm	s	—	—	dyne	$g_c = 1$

CHAPTER 2

PROPERTIES AND STATES OF A PURE SUBSTANCE

2.1 THE PURE SUBSTANCE

The term "pure substance" designates a substance which is homogeneous throughout and has the same chemical composition from one phase to another.

Water is a pure substance since its chemical composition is the same in all phases. A mixture of gases can be considered a pure substance. But if the mixture is cooled, the new phase would have a different composition from the old and the system would no longer be a pure substance.

2.2 P-V-T BEHAVIOR OF A PURE SUBSTANCE

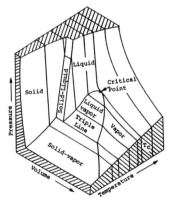

Fig. 2.1 p-v-T Surface for a Substance that contracts on Freezing

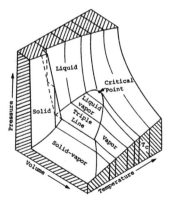

Fig. 2.2 p-v-T Surface for a Substance that expands on Freezing

7

Figures 2.1 and 2.2 are schematic diagrams of the P-V-T surface for a pure substance. They clearly show that a pure substance can exist only in the vapor, liquid or solid phase for certain ranges. To these diagrams, the following terms apply:

a) Critical point is the point beyond which there is no latent heat of vaporization and no other characteristics which normally works a change in phase.

b) The pressure, temperature and specific volume at the critical point are known as the critical pressure P_c, the critical temperature T_c and the critical specific volume V_c.

c) In the liquid-vapor region, the vapor in an equilibrium mixture is called a saturated vapor, and the liquid, a saturated liquid.

d) Saturation temperature is one at which vaporization takes place at a given pressure (called the saturation pressure).

2.3 P-T PROGRAM

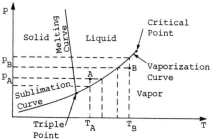

Fig. 2.4 p-T Diagram for a Substance That Expands on Freezing

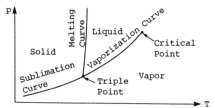

Fig. 2.3 p-T Diagram for a Substance That Contracts on Freezing

8

To these diagrams, the following terms apply:

a) Triple point
   The point at which all three phases can coexist in equilibrium.

b) Sublimation Curve
   The curve along which the solid phase may exist in equilibrium with the vapor phase.

c) Vaporization Curve
   The curve along which the liquid phase may exist in equilibrium with the vapor phase.

d) Melting Curve or Fusion Curve
   The curve along which the solid phase may exist in equilibrium with the liquid phase.

e) State A (shown in Fig. 2.4) is known as a subcooled liquid or a compressed liquid.
   State B (also shown in Fig. 2.4) is known as a superheated vapor.

f) A transition from one solid phase to another is called an allotropic transformation.

2.4 T-V PROGRAM

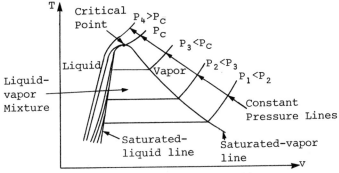

Fig. 2.5 Vapor Dome on a T-v Diagram

2.5 P-V DIAGRAM

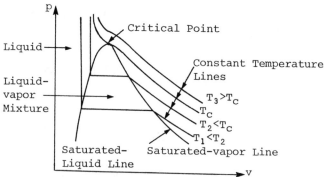

Fig 2.6 Vapor Dome on a p-v Digram

2.6 T-S DIAGRAM

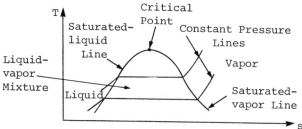

Fig 2.7 Vapor Dome on a T-s Diagram

2.6.1 LATENT HEAT OF VAPORIZATION

The change in enthalpy between the liquid phase and the vapor phase.

2.6.2 LATENT HEAT OF FUSION

The change in enthalpy between the solid phase and the liquid phase.

2.7 H-S DIAGRAM

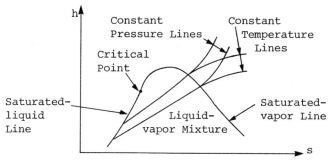

Fig. 2.8 Vapor Dome on an h-s (Mollier) Diagram

2.8 P-H DIAGRAM

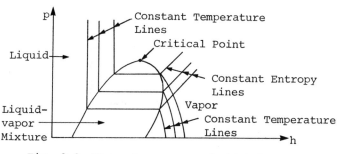

Fig. 2.9 Vapor Dome on a p-h (Mollier) Diagram

2.9 TABLES OF THERMODYNAMIC PROPERTIES

Tables of thermodynamic properties of many substances are available. They consist principally of tabulations of specific volume, enthalpy, and internal energy.

11

The notations commonly used for the properties listed in thermodynamics tables are:

s = Saturated

f = Saturated liquid

g = Saturated vapor or gas

sf = Fusion

fg = Vaporization

sg = Sublimation

From our study of thermodynamic diagrams, we've seen that the data we need may be given in the following tables:

I. Table for Saturated Liquids

II. Table for Saturated Vapors

III. Table for Superheated Vapors

IV. Table for Compressed Liquids

2.9.1 QUALITY

The quality of a substance is defined as:

$$x = \frac{m_g}{m_g + m_f} = \frac{m_{vapor}}{m_{total}}$$

where

m_g = Mass of vapor

m_f = Mass of liquid

2.9.2 MOISTURE

The moisture of a substance is defined as:

$$y = \frac{m_f}{m_f + m_g} = \frac{m_f}{m} = 1 - x$$

where

m_f = Mass of liquid

m_g = Mass of vapor

c) Each property for a substance having a given quality can be found by the equation:

$$P = P_f + x\, P_{fg} = xP_g + (1-x)P_f$$

where

P = Any property (v, u, h, s)

x = Quality

CHAPTER 3

WORK AND HEAT

3.1 DEFINITION OF WORK

The work W done by a force F, when the point of application of the force undergoes a displacement of dx, is defined as:

$$W = \int_1^2 F \, dx$$

(3.1)

3.2 THERMODYNAMIC WORK

When looking at thermodynamics from a microscopic point of view, it is advantageous to relate the definition of work to the concepts of system, property and process. We therefore define work in the following manner: Work is an interaction between a system and its surroundings, and is said to be "done" by a system if the sole effect in the surrounds could be the raising of a weight.

Work done by a system is considered positive and work done on a system is considered negative. Let us illustrate the definition of work with an example.

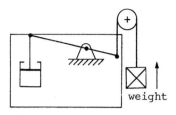

Fig. 3.1

A weight is raised by means of a cord wrapped around an external frictionless pulley, which is connected to a mechanism inside the box (system). Assume weightless links and cord.

3.3 WORK DONE ON A SIMPLE COMPRESSIBLE SYSTEM

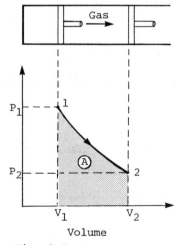

Fig. 3.2

Consider as a system the gas contained in a cylinder as shown in fig. 3.2.

For any small expansion in which the gas increases in volume by dv, the work done by the gas is

15

$$W = \int_1^2 pdv$$

where p is the pressure exerted on the piston.

The interval $\int_1^2 pdv$ is the area under the curve on the P-V diagram. Since we can go from state 1 to state 2 along many different paths, it is evident that the amount of work involved in each case is a function not only of the end states of the process, but it is also dependent on the path that is followed in going from one state to another. For this reason, work is called a path function, or in mathematical language, work is an inexact differential.

3.4 OTHER MODES OF THERMODYNAMIC WORK

In the preceding section, we considered work in P-V-T systems. Work in different kinds of systems is also important. Several different kinds of work are summarized below:

I. Stretched wire work

$$_1W_2 = - \int_1^2 Tdl$$

(3.3)

where T = Tension
dl = change of length of the wire

II. Surface film work

$$_1W_2 = -\int_1^2 y\,dA$$

(3.4)

where

y = Surface Tension
dA = Change of area

III. Magnetic work

$$_1W_2 = \int_1^2 \mu_0 Hd1VM$$

(3.5)

where

μ_0 = Permeability

V = Volume

H = Intensity of the magnetic field

M = Magnetization

IV. Electrical work

$$_1W_2 = \int_1^2 Edz$$

(3.6)

where

E = Electric field
dz = Amount of electrical energy flow into the system

3.5 HEAT

Heat is defined as the form of energy that is transferred across the boundary of a system at a given temperature to another system at a lower temperature by virtue of the temperature difference between the two systems.

Positive heat transfer is heat addition to a system and negative heat transfer is heat rejection by the system.

3.6 COMPARISON OF HEAT AND WORK

There are many similarities between heat and work, and these are summarized here:

a) Heat and work are transient phenomena. Systems never possess heat or work. Heat and work, only cross system boundaries when systems undergo changes of state.

b) Both heat and work are boundary phenomena. Both are observed only at the boundaries of systems, and both represent energy crossing boundaries.

c) Both heat and work are path functions and inexact differentials.

3.7 UNITS OF WORK AND HEAT

	International System	English Engineering System	
Work	Joule (J)*, 1(J) = 1(N)/ (m)	(FT-LBF)	(BTU)*
Power	Watt (W), 1(W) = 1(J)/ (sec)	(FT-LBF) (sec)	(BTU) (sec)
Heat	The units for heat, and for any other forms of energy, are the same as the units for work.		

*Joule is defined as the amount of energy needed to raise a weight; that is, the product of a unit force (one Newton) acting through a unit distance (one meter).

*BTU is defined as the amount of energy required to raise 1 lbm of water from 59.5°F to 60.5°F.

CHAPTER 4

ENERGY AND THE FIRST LAW OF THERMODYNAMICS

4.1 ENERGY OF A SYSTEM

Since for a given closed system, the work done is the same in all adiabatic processes between the equilibrium states, it follows that a property of the system can be defined such that the change between any two equilibrium states is equal to the adiabatic work. We define this property as the energy E of the system or

$$\Delta E = E_2 - E_1 = W_{adiabatic}$$

(4.1)

For a system we would write,

E = Internal energy + Kinetic energy + Potential energy
where:

a) Internal energy (U) is an extensive property, since it depends upon the mass of the system it represents energy modes on the microscopic level, such as energy associated with nuclear spin, molecular binding, magnetic dipole moment and so on.

b) Kinetic energy (K.E.) is the kind of energy that a body has because of its motion. The kinetic energy of a system having a mass m with a velocity v is given by

$$KE = \tfrac{1}{2}mv^2$$

(4.2)

c) Potential energy (P.E.) is the kind of energy that a body has because of its position in a potential field. The potential energy of a system having a mass m, and an elevation z, above a defined plane in a gravitational field with a constant g is given by

$$PE = mgz \qquad (4.3)$$

4.2 THE FIRST LAW OF THERMODYNAMICS

The principle of conservation of energy, the first law of thermodynamics, may simply be stated as:

change in stored energy = energy input - energy output

4.3 THE FIRST LAW FOR A SYSTEM UNDERGOING A CYCLE

Observations have led to the formulation of the first law of thermodynamics which in equation form is written:

$$J \oint dQ = \oint dW \qquad (4.4)$$

where

$\oint dQ$ = Cyclic integral of the heat transfer

$\oint dW$ = Cyclic integral of the work

J = Proportionality factor

4.4 THE FIRST LAW FOR A CHANGE IN THE STATE OF A SYSTEM

For a system undergoing a cycle, changing from state 1 to state 2, we have:

$$dQ - dW = dE \qquad (4.5)$$

where

Q = Heat transferred to the system during the process

W = Work transferred from the system during the process

E is the total energy of the system.

The integrated form of (4.5) with g constant becomes:

$$_1Q_2 - {_1}W_2 = U_2 - U_1 + \frac{m(v_2^2 - v_1^2)}{2} + mg(z_2 - z_1) \qquad (4.6)$$

where

$_1Q_2$ = Change of heat from state 1 to state 2

$U_2 - U_1$ = change in internal energy

$m(v_2^2 - v_1^2)/2$ = Change in kinetic energy

$mg(z_2 - z_1)$ = Change in potential energy

$_1W_2$ = Work done by or in the system

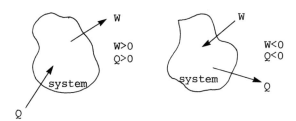

W>0
Q>0

W<0
Q<0

system

system

Q

Q

Fig. 4.1 Signs of work and heat related
with a system*

Notes:

   I. E depends only on the initial and final states and not on the path followed between the two states; therefore, E is a point function and is considered the differential of a property of the systems.

II. The net change of the energy of the system is always equal to the net transfer of energy across the system boundary as heat and work.

III. Equation (4.6) gives only changes in internal energy, both kinetic and potential. We cannot learn absolute value of these quantities from the equation.

IV. Equation (4.5) is a consequence of the first law, and not the first law itself. The first law includes the additional information that energy E is a property.

V. The first step for applying equation (4.6) to the solution of any problem must be the description of a closed system and its boundaries.

*This sign convention is not a universal convention.

4.5 THE THERMODYNAMIC PROPERTY, ENTHALPY

It is convenient to define a new extensive property, enthalpy, as

$$\boxed{H = U + PV}$$

(4.7)

or, per unit mass,

$$h = u + Pv$$

(4.8)

H,h = Enthalpy

U,u = Internal energy

P = Pressure

V,$\bar{v}$ = Volume, Specific Volume

4.6 THE CONSTANT-VOLUME AND CONSTANT-PRESSURE SPECIFIC HEATS

a) $Cv = \left(\dfrac{\delta u}{\delta T}\right)_V$ Constant-volume specific heat   (4.9)

b) $Cp = \left(\dfrac{\delta h}{\delta T}\right)_p$ Constant-pressure specific heat   (4.10)

4.7 CONTROL VOLUME

A control volume is any specified volume in a fixed region in space through which fluid flow takes place. Its surface is called the control surface.

4.8 LAW OF CONSERVATION OF MASS

For any system the law of conservation of mass states that:

mass added - mass removed = change in mass storage.

4.9 CONSERVATION OF MASS FOR AN OPEN SYSTEM

$$\dot{m}_{out} - \dot{m}_{in} = \frac{dm}{dt}$$ (4.11)

where

$\dot{m}_{out}$ = Mass flow out of the control volume

$\dot{m}_{in}$ = Mass flow into the control volume

$\dfrac{dm}{dt}$ = Rate of change in the mass within the control volume

$$g_c = \frac{1 \text{ slug-ft}}{lbf - sec^2}$$

4.10 THE FIRST LAW OF THERMO-DYNAMICS FOR A CONTROL VOLUME

The rate equation of the first law for a control volume is:

$$\dot{Q}_{cv} - \dot{W}_{cv} = \frac{dEcv}{dt} + \Sigma \dot{m}_e (h_e + \frac{v_e^2}{2} + gz_e) - \Sigma \dot{m}_i (h_i + \frac{v_i^2}{2} + gz_i) \quad (4.12)$$

where

$\dot{Q}_{cv}$ = Rate of heat transfer into the control volume.

$\dot{W}_{cv}$ = Work that is associated with the displacement of the control surface and that crosses the surface.

$\Sigma \dot{m}_i (hi + \frac{v_i^2}{2} + gzi)$ = Rate of energy flowing as a result of mass transfer *IN*

$\Sigma \dot{m}_e (h_e + \frac{v_e^2}{2} + gz_e)$ = Rate of energy flowing out as a result of mass transfer

$\frac{dEcv}{dt}$ = Rate of change of energy inside the CV.

$h = u + pv$

$E_{C.V} = \int_V e\rho dv$

$e = u + \frac{v^2}{2g_c} + z\frac{g}{g_c}$

$= (h - pv + \frac{v^2}{2g_c} + z\frac{g}{g_c})$

4.11 THE STEADY-STATE STEADY-FLOW PROCESS (SSSF)

Let us consider the following assumptions:

I. The control volume does not move relative to the coordinate frame.

II. The state of the mass at each point in the CV does not vary with time.

III. The mass flux does not vary with time.

IV. The rates at which heat and work cross the control surface remain constant.

These assumptions lead to a reasonable model which is called the steady-state, steady-flow process (SSSF).

For this type of process we can write:

Continuity equation $\quad \dot{m}_i = \dot{m}_e = \dot{m} \qquad \dfrac{d E.CV}{dt} = 0 \qquad$ (4.13)

First Law

$$\dot{Q}_{cv} - \dot{W}_{cv} = \dot{m}(h_e + \frac{v_e^2}{2} + gz_e) - \dot{m}(h_i + \frac{v_i^2}{2} + gz_i) \quad (4.14)$$

4.12 THE JOULE-THOMSON COEFFICIENT AND THE TROTTLING PROCESS

a) The Joule-Thomas coefficient is defined as

$$\mu_J = \left(\frac{\delta T}{\delta P}\right)_h \qquad (4.15)$$

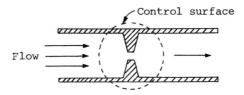

Fig. 4.2 The throttling process

Consider the throttling process in (Fig. 4.2), which is a SSSF process across a restriction, resulting in a drop in pressure. For such a process the μ_J is significant. A positive μ_J means that the temperature drops during throttling, and when μ_J is negative the temperature rises, during throttling.

b) The isothermal Joule-Thomson coefficient is defined as:

$$\mu_J = \left(\frac{\delta h}{\delta P}\right)_t \qquad (4.16)$$

4.13 THE UNIFORM-STATE UNIFORM FLOW PROCESS (USUF)

Let us consider the following assumptions:

I. The cv remains constant relative to the coordinate frame.

II. The state of mass may change with time in the cv, but at any instant of time the state is uniform throughout the entire CV.

III. The state of the mass crossing all the areas of flow is constant in respect to the control surface but the mass flow rates may vary with time.

These assumptions lead to a model which is called a uniform-state, uniform-flow process (USUF).

For this type of process we can write:

Continuity equation (For a period of time t)

$$(m_2 - m_1)_{CV} + \Sigma m_e - \Sigma m_i = 0 \qquad (4.17)$$

First Law

$$Q_{cv} - W_{cv} = \Sigma m_e (h_e + \frac{v_e^2}{2} + gz_e) - \Sigma m_i (h_i + \frac{v_i^2}{2} + gz_i)$$

$$+ \left[m_2(u_2 + \frac{v_2^2}{2} + gz) - m_1(u_1 + \frac{v_1^2}{2} + gz_1) \right]_{cv}$$

$$(4.18)$$

CHAPTER 5

ENTROPY AND THE SECOND LAW OF THERMODYNAMICS

5.1 THE HEAT ENGINE

A heat engine is a system which operates in a cycle while only heat and work cross its boundaries.

A steam power plant is a heat engine which receives heat from a high-temperature system at the boiler, rejects heat to a lower-temperature system at the condenser, and delivers useful work.

5.2 HEAT ENGINE EFFICIENCY

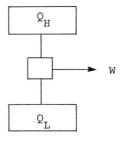

Fig. 5.1

a) We define the efficiency of a work producing heat engine as the ratio of the net work delivered to the environment, to the heat received from the source:

$$\eta = \frac{W}{Q_H} = \frac{Q_H - Q_L}{Q_H} = 1 - \frac{Q_L}{Q_H}$$

(5.1)

where Q_H = Amount of heat added to an engine

Q_L = Amount of heat rejected by an engine

W = Net amount of work produced by an engine

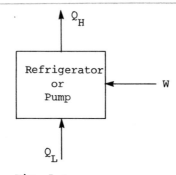

Fig. 5.2

b) Refrigerators and heat pumps are simply heat engines operating in reverse. The concept of coefficient of performance is used in these cases. The coefficient of performance of a refrigerator is given by:

$$\beta_R = \frac{Q_L}{W} = \frac{Q_L}{Q_H - Q_L} = \frac{1}{\dfrac{Q_H}{Q_L} - 1}$$

(5.2)

and the coefficient of performance of a heat pump is given by:

$$\beta_{HP} = \frac{Q_H}{W} = \frac{Q_H}{Q_H - Q_L} = \frac{1}{1 - \dfrac{Q_L}{Q_H}}$$

(5.3)

28

where Q_L = Amount of heat transferred from a low-temperature reservoir

Q_H = Amount of heat transferred to a warmer body

W = Net amount of work required

The expressions for the thermal efficiencies of heat engines, if they are reversible, are given by the following relations:

$$\eta_{th} = 1 - \frac{T_L}{T_H} \qquad (5.4)$$

refrigerator → $$\beta_R = \frac{1}{\frac{T_H}{T_L} - 1} \qquad (5.5)$$

heat pump → $$\beta_{HP} = \frac{1}{1 - \frac{T_L}{T_H}} \qquad (5.6)$$

where T_L = Low temperature heat reservoir

T_H = High temperature heat reservoir

T_H, T_L = Absolute temperatures

Notes

a) The efficiency of a work-producing heat engine operating between two systems is always less than unity, or

$$\eta_{th} < 1.$$

b) The efficiency of any irreversible heat engine is less than that of any reversible engine, or

$$\eta_I \leq \eta_R.$$

c) For any reversible heat engine the net work and net heat in a cycle are zero:

$$\oint_{rev} dQ = \oint_{rev} dW = 0 \qquad (5.7)$$

5.3 THE SECOND LAW

There are two classical statements of the second law:

5.3.1 KELVIN-PLANK STATEMENT

It is impossible to construct a device that will operate in a cycle and produce no effect other than the raising of a weight and the exchange of heat with a single reservoir.

5.3.2 CLAUSIUS STATEMENT

It is impossible to construct a device that operates in a cycle and produces no effect other than the transfer of heat from a cooler body to a hotter body.

5.4 PERPETUAL MOTION MACHINES

5.4.1 PERPETUAL MOTION MACHINE OF THE FIRST KIND (PMM1)

A PMM1 is defined as any system which undergoes a cycle and has no external effect except the raising of a weight.

5.4.2 PERPETUAL MOTION MACHINE OF THE SECOND KIND (PMM2)

A PMM2 is defined as any cyclic device which has heat interactions with a single system, and delivers work.

Notes:

a) A corollary of the first law is that a PMM1 is impossible.

b) A corollary of the second law is that a PMM2 is impossible.

c) The efficiencies of PMM1 and PMM2 are equal to unity.

5.5 THE CARNOT CYCLE

By combining several reversible processes for a system, we may construct a reversible heat engine. The Carnot engine is an example of such an engine. When a large heat reservoir is brought into heat communication with a cylinder containing a certain amount of air confined by a piston, the following processes take place:

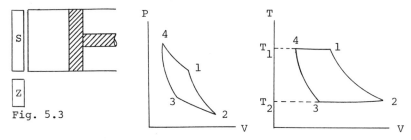

Fig. 5.3

Process 1-2

A reversible adiabatic process in which the temperature of the working fluid decreases from the high temperature to the low temperature

Process 2-3

A reversible isothermal process in which heat is transferred to or from the low-temperature reservoir

Process 3-4

A reversible adiabatic process in which the temperature of the working fluid increases from the low temperature to the high temperature

Process 4-1

A reversible isothermal process in which heat is transferred to or from the high-temperature reservoir

5.6 THERMODYNAMIC TEMPERATURE SCALES

The second law permits the definition of a temperature scale. Such a scale can be defined as follows:

Let us consider a system A (Fig. 5.4) in a state of equilibrium, and a reservoir, R, at constant temperature (for example, the melting point of ice). Operating a heat engine between A and R, the ratio of the heat quantities (Q_A/Q_R) that the engine exchanges with A and R can be evaluated. For a fixed reservoir R at constant temperature T_2, the quantity Q_A/Q_R depends only on the temperature T of system A. Thus

$$\frac{Q_A}{Q_R} = f(T).$$

This can also be expressed in the form,

$$T = F_R \left(\frac{Q_A}{Q_R} \right) \tag{5.8}$$

The function F_R defines a temperature scale which is independent of the nature of any particular thermometric substance and can be determined experimentally.

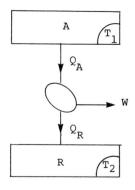

Fig. 5.4

a) The Kelvin scale defined by the relation:

$$T = F_R \left(\frac{Q_A}{Q_R} \right) = -T_R \frac{Q_A}{Q_R}$$

(5.9)

where T_R denotes the temperature in degrees kelvin of a heat reservoir at the triple state of water, $T_R = 273.16$ ^{0}K.

b) Other thermodynamic temperature scales frequently used are the Rankine, Fahrenheit, and Celsius scales. The relations among them are:

$$T(^0K) = t(^0C) + 273.15$$

(5.10)

$$t(^0F) = T(^0R) - 459.67$$

(5.11)

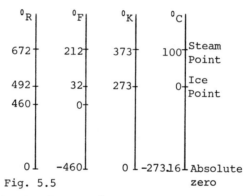

Fig. 5.5

Temperature scales compared at certain identifiable levels of temperature

5.7 ENTROPY

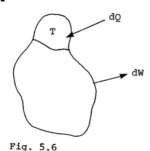

Fig. 5.6

Let us consider a system executing a cyclic reversible process (Fig. 5.6). For this process we define the quantity:

$$dS = \left(\frac{dQ}{T}\right)_{rev} \qquad (5.12)$$

where dQ = Heat supplied to the system

T = Absolute temperature of the system

The quantity dS represents the change in the value of the property of the system, and it is called the entropy.

Notes

a) The equation (5.12) is valid for any reversible process.

b) Entropy is an extensive property, and it is a function of the end points only (a point function).

c) The change in the entropy of a system may be found by integrating (5.12)

$$S_2 - S_1 = \int_1^2 \frac{dQ}{T} \qquad (5.13)$$

5.8 INEQUALITY OF CLAUSIUS

For any irreversible cycle the integral $\oint \frac{dQ}{T}$ is always less than zero,

$$\oint \frac{dQ}{T} < 0 \qquad (5.14)$$

5.9 PRINCIPLE OF THE INCREASE OF ENTROPY

For any isolated system,

$$dS_{isol} \geq 0 \qquad (5.15)$$

a) Principle of the increase of Entropy for a Control Value

$$\frac{dS_{cv}}{dt} + \frac{dS_{surr}}{dt} \geq 0 \qquad (5.16)$$

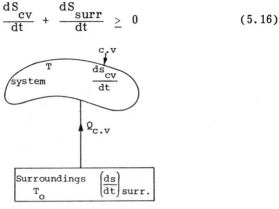

Fig. 5.7 Entropy change for a control volume plus surroundings.

5.10 ENTROPY CHANGE OF A SYSTEM DURING AN IRREVERSIBLE PROCESS

$$dS \geq \frac{dQ}{T} \quad \text{or} \quad S_2 - S_1 \geq \int \frac{dQ}{T} \qquad (5.17)$$

5.11 TWO THERMODYNAMIC RELATIONS

$$TdS = dU + PdV \qquad (5.18)$$

$$TdS = dH - Vdp \qquad (5.19)$$

Equations (5.18) and (5.19) hold for any process, reversible or irreversible, connecting equilibrium states of a simple system.

5.12 THE SECOND LAW OF THERMO-DYNAMICS FOR A CONTROL VOLUME

$$\frac{dS_{cv}}{dt} + \Sigma m_e s_e - \Sigma m_i s_i = \int_A \left(\frac{\dot{Q}_{cv}/A}{T}\right) dA + \int_V \left(\frac{L\dot{W}_{cv}/V}{T}\right) dV \tag{5.20}$$

This expression states that the rate of change of entropy inside the control volume plus the net rate of entropy flow out is equal to the sum of two terms, the integrated heat transfer term and the positive, internal reversibility term.

5.12.1 THE STEADY-STATE STEADY-FLOW PROCESS

For the SSSF, $\dfrac{dS_{cv}}{dt} = 0$.

$$\Sigma m_e s_e - \Sigma m_i s_i - \int_A \left(\frac{\dot{Q}_{cv}/A}{T}\right) dA \tag{5.21}$$

For an adiabatic process, $s_e \geq s_i$.

5.12.2 THE UNIFORM-STATE UNIFORM-FLOW PROCESS

$$\left[m_2 s_2 - m_i s_i\right]_{cv} + \Sigma m_e s_e - \Sigma m_i s_i = \int_0^t \left(\frac{\dot{Q}_{cv} + L\dot{W}_{cv}}{T}\right) dt \tag{5.22}$$

5.12.3 THE REVERSIBLE STEADY-STATE, STEADY FLOW PROCESS

1. For a reversible adiabatic process,

$$W = - \int_i^e VdP + \frac{(v_i^2 - v_e^2)}{2} + g(z_i - z_e) \qquad (5.23)$$

2. If we consider a reversible steady-state, steady-flow process in which the work is zero and the fluid is incompressible, equation (5.23) can be integrated to give,

$$V(P_e - P_i) + \frac{(v_e^2 - v_i^2)}{2} + g(z_e - z_i) = 0 \qquad (5.24)$$

This is known as Bernoulli's equation.

3. For a reversible and isothermal process,

$$T(s_e - s_i) = \frac{\dot{Q}_{cv}}{\dot{m}} = q \qquad (5.25)$$

CHAPTER 6

AVAILABILITY FUNCTIONS

6.1 REVERSIBLE WORK

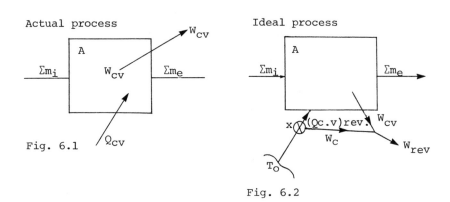

Fig. 6.2

In Fig. 6.1, we consider a system which shows a control volume undergoing a USUF process. There are irreversibilities present as in every actual process. In Fig. 6.2, we imagine an ideal process where all quantities and states are the same as for the actual process. All processes in this case are completely reversible.

The reversible work is determined by the relation:

$$\boxed{W_{rev} = (W_{cv})_{rev} + W_c} \qquad (6.1)$$

where W_{rev} $\equiv$ Reversible work

$(W_{cv})_{rev}$ $\equiv$ Work crossing the control surface for the reversible case.

W_c $\equiv$ Work output of the reversible heat engine X

Q_{cv} $\equiv$ Heat transfer with surroundings at temperature T_0

The difference between the reversible work and the work done in the first case (Fig. 6.1) is called the Irreversibility and is defined,

$$\boxed{I = W_{rev} - W_{cv}}$$ (6.2)

a) The reversible work of a control volume that exchanges heat with the surroundings at temperature T_0 is:

$$W_{rev} = \Sigma m_i (h_i - T_0 s_i + \frac{v_i^2}{2} + gz_i) - \Sigma m_e (h_e - T_0 s_e + \frac{v_e^2}{2} + gz_e)$$

$$- \left[m_2 (u_2 - T_0 s_2 + \frac{v_2^2}{2} + gz_2) - m_1 (u_1 - T_0 s_1 + \frac{v_1^2}{2} + gz_1) \right]_{cv}$$

(6.3)

where:

$\Sigma m_i (h_i - T_0 s_i + \frac{v_i^2}{2} + gz_i)$ = Rate of energy flowing in as a result of mass transfer

$\Sigma m_e (h_e - T_0 s_e + \frac{v_e^2}{2} + gz_e)$ = Rate of energy flowing out as a result of mass transfer

$m_2 (u_2 - T_0 s_2 + \frac{v_2^2}{2} + gz_2)$ = State within the control volume at state 2

$m_1 (u_1 - T_0 s_1 + \frac{v_1^2}{2} + gz_1)$ = State within the control volume at state 1

1. For a system with fixed mass, the reversible work is:

39

$$\left(\frac{W_{rev}}{m}\right)_{1\ 2} = {}_1W_{rev\ 2} = \left[(u_1 - T_0 s_1 + \frac{v_1^{\ 2}}{2} + gz_1)\right.$$

$$\left. - (u_2 - T_0 s_2 + \frac{v_2^{\ 2}}{2} + gz_2)\right] \qquad (6.4)$$

2. For a steady-state, steady-flow process the reversible work is:

$$W_{rev} = \Sigma m_i(h_i - T_0 s_i + \frac{v_i^{\ 2}}{2} + gz_i) - \Sigma m_e(h_e - T_0 s_e + \frac{v_e^2}{2} + gz_e) \qquad (6.5)$$

b) The irreversibility of a control volume that exchanges heat with the surroundings at temperature T_0 is:

$$I = \Sigma m_e T_0 s_e - \Sigma m_i T_0 s_i + m_2 T_0 s_1 - T_0 s_1 - Q_{cv} \qquad (6.6)$$

1. For a system with fixed mass, we have from above:

$$_1 I_2 = m T_0(s_2 - s_1) - {}_1 Q_2 \qquad (6.7)$$

2. For the steady-state, steady-flow process ($m_2 T_0 s_2 = m_1 T_0 s_1$):

$$I = \Sigma m_e T_0 s_e - \Sigma m_i T_0 s_i - Q_{cv} \qquad (6.8)$$

6.2 AVAILABILITY

The maximum reversible work that can be done by a system in a given state is called availability, and is defined (per unit mass in the absence of kinetic and potential energy):

$$\phi = (W_{rev})_{max} - W_{surr} \qquad (6.9)$$

where

$$(W_{rev})_{max} = (u - T_0 s) - (u_0 - T_0 s_0)$$

$$W_{surr} = P_0(V_0 - V) = -m P_0(v - v_0)$$

$$\therefore \quad \phi = (u-u_0) + P_0(v-v_0) - T_0(s-s_0) \qquad (6.10)$$

where   u = Internal energy of the system

   v = Specific volume of the system

   s = Entropy of the system

u_0, v_0, s_0 = Internal energy, specific volume, and entropy of the surroundings

CHAPTER 7

GASES

7.1 GAS CONSTANT

It has been found experimentally that for all homogeneous simple systems the ratio $\frac{PV}{T}$ approaches a finite limit as the pressure approaches zero. This limit is known as the gas constant R:

$$R = \lim_{P \to 0} \left(\frac{PV}{T} \right) \qquad (7.1)$$

7.1.1 UNIVERSAL GAS CONSTANT

The universal gas constant $\bar{R}$ is defined by the relation:

$$\bar{R} = 32 \, R_{O_2} \qquad (7.2)$$

where R_{O_2} = gas constant of atmospheric oxygen.

The value of the universal gas constant, as determined experimentally, is as follows:

$\bar{R} = 1.9859$ cal$/^0$K g-mole, Btu$/^0$R lb-mole

$= 82.06$ cm^3 atm$/^0$K g-mole

$= 83.15$ cm^3 bar$/^0$K g-mole

$$= 0.8478 \text{ kg m} / ^{0}\text{K g-mole}$$

$$= 1545.3 \text{ ft lbf} / ^{0}\text{R lb-mole}.$$

The gas constant R is related to the universal gas constant $\overline{R}$ through its molecular weight M in the following manner:

$$R = \frac{\overline{R}}{M} \tag{7.3}$$

7.2 BOLZMANN'S CONSTANT

The universal gas constant per molecule, usually denoted by K, is called Boltzmann's constant:

$$K = \frac{\overline{R}}{N_0} \tag{7.4}$$

$N_0 = 6.0232 \times 10^{23}$ (Avogadro's number)

7.3 COMPRESSIBILITY

The ratio PV/RT for any simple system is called the compressibility and is denoted z:

$$z = \frac{PV}{RT} \tag{7.5}$$

where   P = Pressure
          V = Volume

R = Universal gas constant

T = Temperature

7.4 SEMIPERFECT GAS

A semiperfect gas is any homogeneous system obeying exactly the following relation for all ranges of pressure and temperature:

$$PV = RT \tag{7.6}$$

7.4.1 PROPERTIES OF A SEMIPERFECT GAS

1. P-V-T Relation

$$PV = RT \tag{7.7}$$

2. Internal Energy

$$u = \int_{T_0}^{T} C_v dT \tag{7.8}$$

3. Enthalpy

$$h = RT_0 + \int_{T_0}^{T} C_p dT \tag{7.9}$$

4. Entropy

$$s - s_0 = \int_{T_0}^{T} C_p \frac{dT}{T} - R \ln \frac{P}{P_0} \qquad (7.10)$$

where subscript ($_0$) refers to an arbitrarily selected state.

5. Specific heat of a semiperfect gas

$$C_v = \frac{1}{K-1} R \qquad\qquad C_p = \frac{K}{K-1} R$$

$$\text{where } K = \frac{C_p}{C_v}$$

7.5 PERFECT GAS (IDEAL GAS)

The perfect gas is a special case of a semiperfect gas obeying the equation,

$$\frac{PV}{RT} = 1 \qquad (7.11)$$

This equation may be written in the following alternative forms:

$$PV = n\bar{R}T$$
$$PV = mRT$$

$$(7.12)$$
$$(7.13)$$

where m is the mass, and n is the number of moles.

7.5.1 PROPERTIES OF A PERFECT GAS

1. P-V-T Relation

$$(7.14)$$

$$PV = RT$$

45

2. Internal Energy

$$u = u(T)$$

$$u - u_0 = \int_{T_0}^{T} C_v dT = C_v(T-T_0) \qquad (7.15)$$

3. Enthalpy Change

$$h = h(T)$$

$$h - h_0 = \int_{T_0}^{T} C_p dT = C_p(T-T_0) \qquad (7.16)$$

4. Entropy Change

$$s - s_0 = \int_{T_0}^{T} \frac{C_v dT}{T} + R \ln \frac{v}{v_0} = C_v \ln \frac{T}{T_0} + R \ln \frac{v}{v_0} \qquad (7.17)$$

$$s - s_0 = \int_{T_0}^{T} \frac{C_p dT}{T} - R \ln \frac{p}{p_0} = C_p \ln \frac{P}{P_0} - R \ln \frac{P}{P_0} \qquad (7.18)$$

5. Specific Heats

$$K = K(T) \qquad C_v = C_v(T) \qquad C_p = C_p(T)$$

$$C_p - C_v = R$$

$$C_p = \frac{RK}{K-1}$$

$$C_v = \frac{R}{K-1} \qquad K = \frac{C_p}{C_v}$$

7.5.2 TWO DIAGRAMS FOR A PERFECT GAS

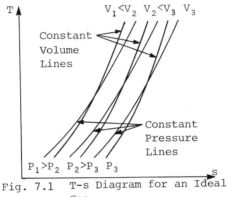

Fig. 7.1   T-s Diagram for an Ideal Gas

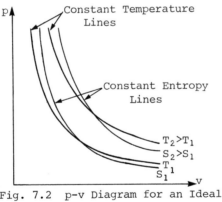

Fig. 7.2   p-v Diagram for an Ideal Gas

a)   The reversible polytropic process for a perfect gas

A reversible polytropic process is one for which the pressure-volume relation is given by the relation,

$$PV^n = \text{constant} \qquad (7.19)$$

The polytropic processes for various values of n are shown on the P-r and T-s diagrams below:

47

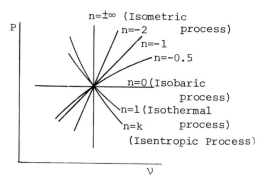

Fig. 7.3 Polytropic processes

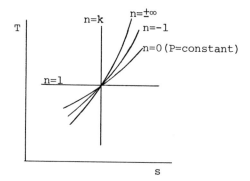

1. For a polytropic process we have the following relations:

$$\frac{T_2}{T_1} = \left(\frac{P_2}{P_1}\right)^{(n-1)/n} = \left(\frac{V_1}{V_2}\right)^{n-1} \qquad (7.20)$$

2. For a system consisting of a perfect gas, the work done at the moving boundary during a reversible polytropic process is:

$$_1W_2 = \frac{P_2 V_2 - P_1 V_1}{1 - n} = \frac{mR(T_2 - T_1)}{1 - n} \qquad (7.21)$$

3. Isentropic process for a perfect gas:

48

$$\frac{T_2}{T_1} = \left(\frac{P_2}{P_1}\right)^{(K-1)/K} = \left(\frac{V_1}{V_2}\right)^{K-1}$$

$$P_1 V_1^K = P_2 V_2^K$$

(7.22)

where $K = C_p / C_v$

7.6 REAL GAS

For a real gas, the value of z may be greater or less than unity. Thus z gives the deviation from perfect gas behavior.

It has been found experimentally that for many gases the compressibility factor z may be approximated by the relation,

$$z = z(p_r, T_R)$$

(7.23)

which is the basis of the generalized compressibility chart in which z versus p_R is given for various values of T_R. This is shown in (Fig. 7.4):

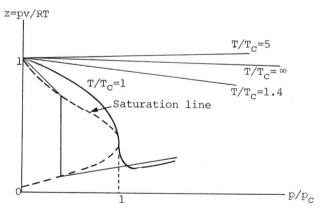

Fig. 7.4 Generalized compressibility chart

where $\qquad P_r = \dfrac{P}{P_c}$ = Reduced pressure,

$\qquad\qquad T_r = \dfrac{T}{T_c}$ = Reduced temperature

$\qquad\qquad P_c$ = Critical pressure

$\qquad\qquad T_c$ = Critical temperature

7.6.1 GENERALIZED ENTHALPY CHART FOR REAL GAS

To use the chart given in Fig. 7.5, all we need to know is the critical pressure p_c and the critical temperature T_c of the gas. Making use of this chart, we may give the change of enthalpy between two states as:

$$\bar{h}_2 - \bar{h}_1 = T_c\left[\left(\frac{\bar{h}^*-\bar{h}}{T_c}\right)_{T_1,P_1} - \left(\frac{\bar{h}^*-\bar{h}}{T_c}\right)_{T_2,P_2}\right]$$

$$+ (\bar{h}^*_{T_2,P_2} - \bar{h}^*_{T_1,P_1}) \qquad (7.24)$$

where

$$\bar{h}^*_{T_2,P_2} - \bar{h}^*_{T_1,P_1} = \int_{T_1}^{T_2} \bar{C}_p{}^* dT \quad \begin{array}{l}\text{is enthalpy change}\\ \text{due to perfect gas}\\ \text{behavior}\end{array}$$

$\bar{C}_p{}^*$ = Ideal gas constant-pressure specific heat as a function of temperature

$\bar{h}^*$ = Enthalpy of the gas at zero pressure and a given temperature

$\bar{h}$ = Enthalpy of the gas at the same temperature and any pressure p.

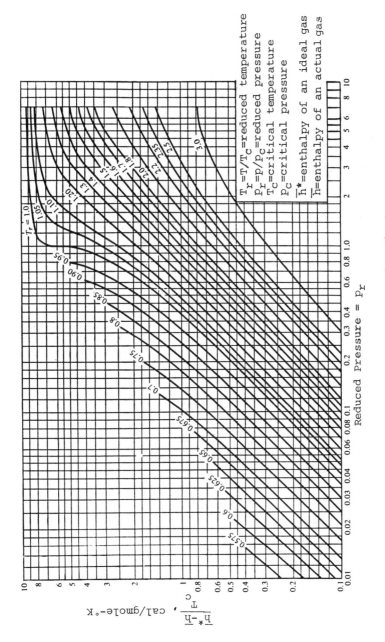

Fig. 7.5 Generalized Enthalpy Correction Chart

$T_r = T/T_c$ = reduced temperature
$p_r = p/p_c$ = reduced pressure
T_c = critical temperature
p_c = critical pressure
$\bar{h}^*$ = enthalpy of an ideal gas
$\bar{h}$ = enthalpy of an actual gas

Reduced Pressure = p_r

$\dfrac{\bar{h}^* - \bar{h}}{T_c}$, cal/gmole-°K

51

7.6.2 GENERALIZED ENTROPY CHART FOR REAL GASES

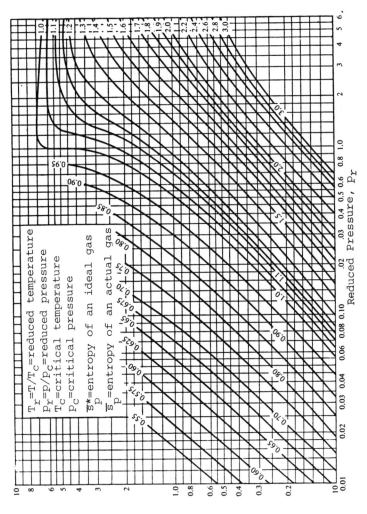

Fig. 7.6 Generalized Entropy Correction Chart

52

Using the generalized entropy correction chart (Fig. 7.6), we can give the change of entropy between two states as:

$$\bar{S}_2 - \bar{S}_1 = (\bar{S}_p^* - \bar{S}_p)_{T_1,P_1} - (\bar{S}_p^* - \bar{S}_p)_{T_2,P_2}$$
$$+ \bar{S}_{T_2,P_2}^* - \bar{S}_{T_1,P_1}^* \tag{7.25}$$

where

$$\bar{S}_{T_2,P_2}^* - \bar{S}_{T_1,P_1}^* = \int_{T_1}^{T_2} \bar{C}_p^* \frac{dT}{T} - \bar{R}\ln\frac{p_2}{p_1}$$

is the entropy change due to perfect gas behavior.

7.6.3 RESIDUAL VOLUME

A useful parameter in describing the behavior of a real gas relative to the ideal gas is the residual volume α, which is defined,

$$\alpha = \frac{\bar{R}T}{P} - \bar{v} \tag{7.26}$$

We note that α is always zero for an ideal gas.

HANDBOOK AND GUIDE FOR
COMPARING and SELECTING
COMPUTER LANGUAGES

BASIC	PL/1
FORTRAN	APL
PASCAL	ALGOL-60
COBOL	C

- This book is the first of its kind ever produced in computer science.

- It examines and highlights the differences and similarities among the eight most widely used computer languages.

- A practical guide for selecting the most appropriate programming language for any given task.

- Sample programs in all eight languages are written and compared side-by-side. Their merits are analyzed and evaluated.

- Comprehensive glossary of computer terms.

Available at your local bookstore or order directly from us by sending in coupon below.

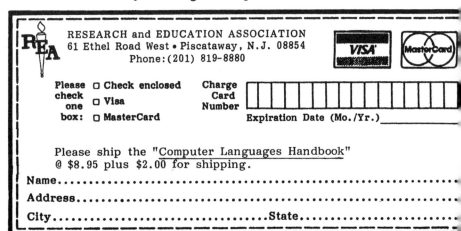

RESEARCH and EDUCATION ASSOCIATION
61 Ethel Road West • Piscataway, N.J. 08854
Phone:(201) 819-8880

VISA   MasterCard

Please check one box:
☐ Check enclosed
☐ Visa
☐ MasterCard

Charge Card Number

Expiration Date (Mo./Yr.) _____

Please ship the "Computer Languages Handbook" @ $8.95 plus $2.00 for shipping.

Name..

Address..

City...State.....................

THE PROBLEM SOLVERS

The "PROBLEM SOLVERS" are comprehensive supplemental textbooks designed to save time in finding solutions to problems. Each "PROBLEM SOLVER" is the first of its kind ever produced in its field. It is the product of a massive effort to illustrate almost any imaginable problem in exceptional depth, detail, and clarity. Each problem is worked out in detail with step-by-step solution, and the problems are arranged in order of complexity from elementary to advanced. Each book is fully indexed for locating problems rapidly.

ADVANCED CALCULUS
ALGEBRA & TRIGONOMETRY
AUTOMATIC CONTROL
  SYSTEMS/ROBOTICS
BIOLOGY
BUSINESS, ACCOUNTING,
  & FINANCE
CALCULUS
CHEMISTRY
COMPLEX VARIABLES
COMPUTER SCIENCE
DIFFERENTIAL EQUATIONS
ECONOMICS
ELECTRICAL MACHINES
ELECTRIC CIRCUITS
ELECTROMAGNETICS
ELECTRONIC COMMUNICATIONS
ELECTRONICS
FINITE and DISCRETE MATH
FLUID MECHANICS/DYNAMICS
GENETICS

GEOMETRY:
  PLANE • SOLID • ANALYTIC
HEAT TRANSFER
LINEAR ALGEBRA
MACHINE DESIGN
MECHANICS: STATICS • DYNAMICS
NUMERICAL ANALYSIS
OPERATIONS RESEARCH
OPTICS
ORGANIC CHEMISTRY
PHYSICAL CHEMISTRY
PHYSICS
PRE-CALCULUS
PSYCHOLOGY
STATISTICS
STRENGTH OF MATERIALS &
  MECHANICS OF SOLIDS
TECHNICAL DESIGN GRAPHICS
THERMODYNAMICS
TRANSPORT PHENOMENA:
  MOMENTUM • ENERGY • MASS
VECTOR ANALYSIS

If you would like more information about any of these books, complete the coupon below and return it to us or go to your local bookstore.